LionHouse
Pies

OTHER LION HOUSE COOKBOOKS

Lion House Bakery

Lion House Christmas

Lion House Classics

Lion House Weddings

Pies

Compiled by
Brenda Hopkin

DESERET
BOOK
Salt Lake City, Utah

Design and photo art direction by Shauna Gibby
Photographs on pages 4, 9, 14, 19, 20, 31, 36, 43, 46, 50, 53, 56, 64, 81, 82, 90, 109
   by Robert Casey
Photographs on pages 49, 89, 95, 96 by John Luke
Photographs on pages 32, 35, 77, 104 by Alan Blakely
Photographs on pages 26, 61 by Ramon Winegar
Food styling by Maxine Bramwell

Visit us at DeseretBook.com

Library of Congress Cataloging-in-Publication Data
Hopkin, Brenda.
   Lion House pies / compiled by Brenda Hopkin.
      p. cm.
   Includes index.
   ISBN 978-1-60641-827-7 (hardbound : alk. paper)
   1. Pies.   2. Lion House (Restaurant)   I. Title.
   TX773.H66 2010
   641.8'652—dc22   2010022506

Printed in China
R. R. Donnelley, Shenzhen, China

10 9 8 7 6 5 4 3 2 1

Contents

Introduction

From 1856 to the present, the Lion House has been baking a wide variety of goods for the enjoyment of all those who ever lived in the Lion House or, currently, for those who visit there.

When Brigham Young's family resided in the Lion House, baking the essential breads, pies, cookies, and cakes went on almost around the clock. Approximately seventy-five people needed to be fed three meals a day, and there was only a wood-burning stove to bake everything in. Brigham Young's wives became very skilled at turning out the best baked goods of that day. There were no corner stores to run to if they ran out of bread or needed a dessert to feed unexpected guests.

Today the Lion House Bakery still bakes almost around the clock. The skilled staff takes great pride in providing baked goods for fans throughout Utah, Idaho, Arizona, and Colorado, plus the many new fans who happen to be in the area of the Lion House or one of its pantries in the Deseret Book stores. Of course they don't use a wood-burning stove anymore, but just as much love goes into the baking of each roll, pie, cookie, and cake as it did in Brigham's day.

There are some fun new recipes in *Lion House Pies,* plus some recipes from Lion House cookbooks that are now out of print. There are also several pie crust recipes. All are easy to make, but the Lion House Pie Crust is the easiest. It rolls out and forms into the pans just like sugar cookie dough. For those who have mastered the art of baking pies or want a little more challenge, we have included the Buttermilk Pie Crust and the Old Fashioned Pie Crust recipes.

May all who use this book have many hours of enjoyment in making delicious pies or in finding a new skill—one that will enrich your lives and bring a smile to all who partake of the pies you have made.

As it is with everything we do, making pies requires practice, practice, and practice to get the results you want. Happy baking!

Helpful Tips for Making Pies

- For better sealing, brush edges of pie crusts with water just before putting on top crust.

- For a beautiful golden top, brush pie crust with milk, cream, half-and-half, or evaporated milk and sprinkle with sugar before baking.

- If your oven is large enough, bake 4 to 8 pies at a time and freeze in gallon freezer bags. When pies are frozen, stack them on top of each other. When needed, take prebaked frozen pie out of plastic bag and bake at 325 degrees F. for 35 to 40 minutes.

- Keep pie shells from shrinking by pricking bottoms with a fork before baking. You can also prevent shrinking by lining dough with aluminum foil. Pour 2 to 3 cups dried beans, wheat, or rice into foil-lined shell and bake for half the baking time. Lift out foil and contents and continue baking for remainder of baking time.

- Experiment with different pastry recipes for your pie crusts. You may find that you prefer one over another, or that one tastes best with fruit pies and another tastes better with cream pies.

Oatmeal Crisp Pie Crust (see page 12)

Chapter 1

Pie Crusts

Buttermilk Pie Crust

3 cups flour
½ teaspoon salt
1 cup shortening
¼ cup margarine or butter
½ cup buttermilk
1 tablespoon oil

Place flour and salt in a medium bowl; stir with a fork. Add shortening and margarine and cut together with a pastry blender or two knives until mixture resembles the size of small peas.

Add buttermilk and oil and blend together with a fork or your hands until all the flour is moist. This will make 3 or 4 crusts depending on how thick you like your crust.

If the recipe calls for a baked pie shell, bake at 375 degrees F. for 15 to 18 minutes.

Note: This is a very tender dough. The scraps of dough left after making your first pie may be added back into the rest of the dough. This may be doubled with good success.

Graham Cracker Pie Crust

16 graham cracker squares
3 tablespoons sugar
⅓ cup butter or margarine, melted

Place graham crackers in a plastic bag (8 at a time). Seal bag and roll with rolling pin to make fine crumbs. Pour into a medium bowl and repeat the process with remaining crackers. Add sugar and stir with a fork. Pour the melted butter on top of the crumb mixture. Stir until crumbs are moist. Pour mixture into a 9-inch pie pan and gently press crumbs into the bottom and sides of pan. This crust may be used either chilled or baked. Makes one 9-inch crust.

If the recipe calls for a baked pie shell, bake at 375 degrees F. for 12 minutes.

Pastry for Double-Crust Pie

2½ cups all-purpose flour
¼ cup granulated sugar
½ teaspoon salt
1 cup butter-flavored shortening, chilled
1 egg, beaten
1 tablespoon vinegar
¼ cup ice water

In a medium bowl, mix together flour, sugar, and salt. Cut the shortening into the flour until pea-sized crumbs form. Carefully stir in beaten egg and vinegar. Gently sprinkle in water until dough starts to hold together. Shape dough into 2 balls. Use to make two 9-inch single-crust pies or one double-crust pie.

If the recipe calls for a baked pie shell, roll out dough, press into pie pan, trim and flute edges, prick bottom of shell with a fork, and bake at 375 degrees F. for 15 to 18 minutes.

Apricot Pineapple Pie (see page 39)

Lion House Pie Crust

¼ cup butter
⅓ cup lard
¼ cup margarine
⅓ cup shortening
1 tablespoon granulated sugar
½ teaspoon baking powder
1 teaspoon salt
1 tablespoon nonfat dry milk
1½ cups pastry flour
1½ cups bread flour
½ cup plus 1 tablespoon cold water

In a medium bowl, cream together butter, lard, margarine, and shortening using an electric mixer. In a separate bowl, whisk together sugar, baking powder, salt, and dry milk powder; add to creamed butter mixture and mix briefly. Add pastry flour and beat until blended. Add bread flour and mix slightly. Pour in water and beat again just until water is blended.

Divide dough into 2 or 3 balls. Roll out each ball on a floured board. Line pie pan with dough and cut off excess dough. Flute edges. For recipes that call for baked pie crusts, prick holes in bottom with fork. Bake empty pie shell at 375 degrees F. for 15 to 18 minutes, or until light golden brown. Otherwise, fill unbaked pie shell and bake according to recipe. Makes 2 to 3 9-inch pie shells.

Note: You may substitute 3 cups all-purpose flour for the pastry and bread flour called for in the recipe. Additionally, this dough may also be made by hand-cutting the fats into the dry ingredients. This recipe may be used to make the crust for any recipe in this book that calls for a single- or double-crust pastry.

Lite Pie Crust

⅓ cup margarine, cut in small pieces
1 cup flour
⅓ cup ice water
1 egg white
1½ teaspoons white vinegar
¼ teaspoon salt

In a small bowl, cut margarine into flour with a fork until mixture resembles coarse meal. Combine water, egg white, vinegar, and salt in a small bowl; mix well. Add liquid mixture to flour mixture. Mix lightly with a fork until mixture forms a ball. Refrigerate for at least ½ hour before rolling out dough. Makes one 9-inch pie shell.

For baked pie shell: Roll pastry in a circle; fit into pie pan. Flute edges. Prick in several places with fork. Bake at 375 degrees F. for 15 to 18 minutes or until light golden brown.

Oatmeal Crisp Pie Crust (shown on page 4)

4⅓ cups all-purpose flour
⅔ cup rolled oats (not quick oats)
½ teaspoon baking powder
½ teaspoon salt
1 tablespoon packed brown sugar
1½ cups shortening
½ cup cold unsalted butter, cut into small pieces
1 egg
1 tablespoon vinegar
Ice water

Stir together flour, oats, baking powder, salt, and brown sugar in a large bowl. Cut in shortening with pastry cutter or 2 knives. Add small pieces of butter and set aside. Mix together egg, vinegar, and enough ice water to measure 1 cup. Add to flour mixture. Mix well. Divide into 4 balls. Wrap with plastic wrap and refrigerate until ready to use. Makes enough dough for two 9-inch double-crust pies or 4 single-crust pies.

If the recipe calls for a baked pie shell, bake at 375 degrees F. for 15 to 18 minutes.

Old-Fashioned Pie Crust

4 cups all-purpose flour
1 teaspoon salt
1 cup lard
1 egg, beaten
1 tablespoon vinegar
water

Place flour and salt in a medium bowl and mix together. Add lard and cut in with a pastry blender until the mixture is the size of small peas (or rub the flour and lard together between the palms of your hands).

In a one-cup measuring cup, beat egg with a fork. Add vinegar to the egg and add water to make 1 cup. Stir slightly and pour over first mixture. With a fork stir together until all dry ingredients are stirred in. Makes four 9-inch crusts.

If the recipe calls for a baked pie shell, bake at 375 degrees F. for 15 to 18 minutes.

Five-Step Black Bottom Pie (see page 23)

Chapter 2

Chocolate Pies

Almond Chocolate Pie

1 graham cracker crust or baked 9-inch pie shell (see page 7 or 10)
½ cup almond slivers, toasted
1 (7-ounce) chocolate bar
½ cup half-and-half
18 large marshmallows
1 cup heavy whipping cream

Place almonds on a cookie sheet and bake for 5 to 7 minutes at 350 degrees F. Almonds should be light golden brown. Remove from oven. Be careful not to overcook; almonds will continue to brown after being removed from the oven.

Place the chocolate bar, half-and-half, and marshmallows in the top of a double boiler and heat until chocolate bar and marshmallows are melted. In a large bowl, whip the cream until stiff; fold cream and almonds into chocolate mixture. Pour into crust and refrigerate to cool. When cool, place in freezer. Remove from freezer 1 hour before serving. Makes 1 pie.

Black Forest Pie

1 unbaked 9-inch pie shell (see page 10)

Filling

¾ cup butter or margarine
6 tablespoons unsweetened cocoa
1 cup sugar, divided
⅔ cup ground blanched almonds
2 tablespoons flour
3 eggs, separated
2 tablespoons water

Topping

⅓ cup sour cream
2 tablespoons sugar
½ teaspoon vanilla
1 cup canned cherry pie filling

Glaze

½ cup semisweet chocolate chips
1½ teaspoons shortening

For filling: In a medium saucepan, melt butter or margarine; stir in cocoa and ¾ cup sugar. Remove from heat and allow to cool for 5 minutes. Add almonds and flour; stir well. Add egg yolks one at a time, stirring well after each addition. Stir in water. In a medium bowl, beat egg whites at high speed until foamy. Gradually add ¼ cup sugar, beating all the time, until soft peaks form. Fold chocolate mixture into egg whites just until blended. Pour mixture into unbaked pastry shell. Bake at 350 degrees F. for 35 to 45 minutes or until wooden toothpick inserted in center comes out clean. Cool 5 minutes.

For topping: In a medium bowl, combine sour cream, sugar, and vanilla. Spread over warm pie. Spoon cherry pie filling over the top and return pie to oven for 5 minutes.

For glaze: Melt chocolate chips and shortening over low heat in a small saucepan, stirring constantly. Drizzle over pie and refrigerate for at least 2 hours. Makes 1 pie.

Chocolate Angel Pie

Meringue Shell

2 egg whites, room temperature
⅛ teaspoon salt
⅛ teaspoon cream of tartar
½ cup sugar
½ cup finely chopped nuts
½ teaspoon vanilla

Filling

1½ cups heavy cream
1 teaspoon vanilla
1 (8-ounce) milk chocolate bar with almonds

For meringue shell: In a medium bowl, beat egg whites, salt, and cream of tartar until frothy. Gradually add sugar, beating until stiff peaks form. Fold in nuts and vanilla. Spread into a greased 9-inch pie pan, building up on sides of pan. Bake at 300 degrees F. for 50 minutes. Cool completely.

For filling: Whip cream with vanilla; set aside. Break up three-fourths of the chocolate bar into pieces and melt in top of a double boiler or microwave in a glass bowl. When chocolate is just lukewarm, fold into whipped cream and vanilla. Pile chocolate filling into cooled meringue shell. Grate remaining chocolate to garnish pie. Chill in refrigerator for two hours before serving. Makes 1 pie.

Chocolate Angel Pie

Chocolate Chip Walnut Pie

Chocolate Chip Walnut Pie

1 unbaked 9-inch pie shell (see page 10)
2 eggs
½ cup pastry flour
⅓ cup granulated sugar
⅓ cup packed dark brown sugar
¾ cup butter, melted and cooled
1 cup semisweet chocolate chips
1 cup chopped walnuts

Beat eggs with an electric mixer until foamy. Add flour and sugars and mix well. Stir in cooled melted butter. Fold in chocolate chips and walnuts. Pour into unbaked pie shell.

Bake at 350 degrees F. for 45 minutes, or until golden brown and set in the middle. Cool on a wire rack. Serve warm. Makes 1 pie.

Chocolate Cream Pie

2 baked 9-inch pie shells (see page 10)
4 cups milk, divided
2 cups half-and-half
2 tablespoons butter
1¼ cups granulated sugar, divided
3 egg yolks
¼ teaspoon salt
½ cup cornstarch
1½ teaspoons vanilla
1 to 1⅓ cups semisweet chocolate chips
Whipped cream, for garnish

Place 3 cups milk in top pan of a double boiler; add half-and-half, butter, and ¾ cup sugar and stir. Heat over medium-high heat until butter is melted and milk is scalded.

In a small bowl, whisk egg yolks well; add remaining ½ cup sugar and salt and whisk very well. Slowly add egg mixture to hot milk mixture, stirring constantly for about half a minute; allow mixture to cook for 15 to 20 minutes, stirring frequently. (This gives eggs time to cook and start thickening. Undercooking at this point can slow the finishing process by as much as half an hour.)

Mix 1 cup milk and cornstarch in a small bowl and slowly add to hot mixture, stirring constantly to avoid formation of lumps. Continue stirring for at least 2 minutes, then stir every 5 minutes for 15 to 20 minutes. When pudding is thick, add vanilla and chocolate chips. Stir until chips are melted.

Remove double boiler from stove. Pour half of the filling into each pie shell, rounding tops of pies. Cool on wire racks and then chill in refrigerator 3 to 4 hours. When ready to serve, whip cream and spread over pies. Makes 2 pies.

Five-Step Black Bottom Pie (shown on page 14)

Crust
36 gingersnaps
½ cup melted butter or margarine
Dash salt

Filling
4 cups milk
4 tablespoons butter or margarine
½ cup cornstarch
1½ cups sugar
½ cup water
4 eggs, separated
2 teaspoons vanilla
2 squares unsweetened baking chocolate
2 envelopes (or 2 tablespoons) unflavored gelatin
½ cup cold water
1 cup sugar
1 teaspoon cream of tartar
2 teaspoons imitation rum flavoring
1 cup whipped cream, for garnish
Flakes of chocolate, for garnish

Step 1: Crush gingersnaps; roll fine and combine with ½ cup melted butter or margarine and salt. Mold evenly into 11-inch springform pan.

Step 2: Scald milk; add butter. Combine cornstarch and sugar; moisten with enough water to make a paste. Stir paste into scalded milk and cook until mixture comes to a boil, stirring constantly. Stir hot mixture gradually into slightly beaten egg yolks. Return to heat and cook 2 minutes. Add vanilla. Remove 2 cups of custard; add chocolate and beat well. Pour into crumb crust and chill.

Step 3: Blend gelatin with cold water; allow to sit a few minutes, then fold into remaining hot custard. Cool.

Step 4: Beat egg whites, 1 cup sugar, and cream of tartar into a meringue. Add rum flavoring and fold into custard from step 2.

Step 5: When chocolate custard has set, pour plain custard on top and chill until set. Serve with whipped cream and bits of chocolate for garnish. Makes 1 pie.

German Chocolate Pie

2 baked 9-inch pie shells (see page 10)
4 cups milk, divided
2 cups half-and-half
2 tablespoons butter
1¼ cups granulated sugar, divided
3 egg yolks
¼ teaspoon salt
½ cup cornstarch
1½ teaspoons vanilla
1½ cups semisweet chocolate chips
1 cup coconut
½ cup chopped pecans
½ cup caramel ice cream topping
Whipped cream, for garnish

Place 3 cups milk in top pan of a double boiler; add half-and-half, butter, and ¾ cup sugar and stir. Heat over medium-high heat until butter is melted and milk is scalded.

In a small bowl, whisk egg yolks well; add remaining ½ cup sugar and salt and whisk very well. Slowly add egg mixture to hot milk mixture, stirring constantly for about half a minute; allow mixture to cook for 15 to 20 minutes, stirring frequently. (This gives eggs time to cook and start thickening. Undercooking at this point can slow the finishing process by as much as half an hour.)

Mix 1 cup milk and cornstarch in a small bowl and slowly add to hot mixture, stirring constantly to avoid formation of lumps. Continue stirring for at least 2 minutes and then stir every 5 minutes for 15 to 20 minutes. When pudding is thick, add vanilla, chocolate chips, coconut, pecans, and caramel topping. Stir until well blended and chocolate chips are melted.

Remove double boiler from stove. Pour half of the filling into each pie shell, rounding tops of pies. Cool on wire racks and then chill in refrigerator 3 to 4 hours. When ready to serve, whip cream and spread over pies. Makes 2 pies.

Grasshopper Pie

Crust

1½ cups finely crushed chocolate wafers (25 wafers)
6 tablespoons butter or margarine, melted

Filling

6½ cups miniature marshmallows
½ cup milk
¼ cup crème de menthe syrup
1 cup whipping cream
Few drops green food coloring (optional)
Whipped cream, for garnish
Chocolate curls, for garnish

For crust: Combine crushed wafers and melted butter. Spread evenly on bottom and sides of 9-inch pie pan. Chill about 1 hour.

For filling: In large saucepan, combine marshmallows and milk. Cook over low heat until marshmallows are melted. Remove from heat and cool, stirring several times while cooling. Add crème de menthe. Whip cream and fold into marshmallow mixture. Add food coloring, if desired.

Pour filling into crust. Chill 2 hours before serving. Garnish with whipped cream and chocolate curls. Makes 1 pie.

Very Berry Pie (see page 55)

Chapter 3

Fruit Pies, Tarts, and Crisps

Assembling and Baking Fruit Pies

To assemble a fruit pie, line a 9-inch pie pan with dough, pressing dough lightly against sides of pan and letting dough hang over edges of pie pan.

Spoon pie filling into unbaked shell. Brush edge of dough with water and place top crust on pie. Seal crusts together by gently pressing around the edge of pie pan. Cut excess dough from edge of pie. Crimp or flute edges if desired.

Brush crust (but not edge) with milk, cream, half-and-half, or evaporated milk. Vent top crust and then sprinkle sugar on top. Bake at 375 degrees F. for 45 to 50 minutes, or until crust is golden brown.

If crust cracks open or filling comes out the sides, the pie is overdone.

Apple Pie

Pastry for 9-inch double-crust pie (see page 8)
¾ to 1 cup granulated sugar
2 tablespoons all-purpose flour
½ to 1 teaspoon ground cinnamon
¼ to ½ teaspoon nutmeg
⅛ teaspoon salt
5 to 6 golden delicious apples, peeled, cored, and sliced
2 tablespoons butter or margarine

Roll out pastry for bottom crust and line bottom and sides of pie pan. Roll out top crust, fold in half, and cut three ½-inch slits through both layers of crust, then set aside. In a large bowl, combine dry ingredients and stir. Place sliced apples on top of dry ingredients and stir. Pour apple mixture into bottom of crust. Dot with small pieces of butter.

Moisten edge of pie crust with water. Place top crust on pie and seal. Brush with milk, sprinkle with sugar, and bake at 375 degrees F. for 45 to 50 minutes or until apples test tender when a sharp knife is inserted into vent hole in top crust. Makes 1 pie.

Note: A 30-ounce can of apple pie filling may be substituted for fresh apples, sugar, flour, and salt. Pour filling into pie crust. Sprinkle with cinnamon and nutmeg and dot with butter. Follow directions above for finishing pie.

Caramel Apple Pie

Pastry for 9-inch double-crust pie (see page 8)
¾ cup granulated sugar, plus additional for dusting top crust
½ cup all-purpose flour
1 teaspoon ground cinnamon, plus additional for dusting top crust
½ teaspoon kosher salt
½ teaspoon nutmeg
8 apples, peeled, cored, and sliced
1 tablespoon vanilla
2 tablespoons unsalted butter
2 tablespoons cream

Caramel Sauce

¼ cup butter
1½ cups brown sugar
½ cup heavy cream
2 tablespoons corn syrup
1 teaspoon vanilla

For filling: In a large bowl, mix together sugar, flour, cinnamon, kosher salt, and nutmeg. Toss in apples and stir in vanilla. Set aside. Stir the apple mixture every 15 to 20 minutes while making the crust.

Once pastry dough is prepared, roll out pastry for bottom crust 3 inches larger than the pie pan. Ease pastry into pan and cut away so only ½ inch is overlapping the edge of the pie pan. Pour apple filling into prepared crust. Dot the butter over the apples. Brush cream around edges of pie crust.

Roll out pastry for top crust, fold in half, and cut three ½-inch slits through both layers of crust. Unfold crust and place over the apples. Trim away extra crust, leaving 1 inch overlapping. Crimp edges of pie. Brush cream over top and sprinkle sugar and cinnamon over top.

Cover the edges of the pie with foil. Bake at 375 degrees F. for 1 hour and 20 minutes, removing the foil from edges after 30 minutes and covering the whole pie with foil for the last 20 minutes. Pie should be light brown. Cool on a rack for 1 hour. Makes 1 pie. While pie is baking, make the caramel sauce.

For caramel sauce: In a heavy 2-quart saucepan, melt butter on high heat. Add brown sugar, heavy cream, and corn syrup. Bring to a boil, stirring frequently. Reduce heat to medium, until sauce thickens slightly, about 5 to 7 minutes. Remove from heat and add vanilla. Allow to cool in pan for 15 minutes. Drizzle over warm pie.

Caramel Apple Pie

Harvest Apple Crisp

Harvest Apple Crisp

10 cups peeled and sliced apples
1 cup granulated sugar
1 cup plus 1 tablespoon all-purpose flour, divided
1 teaspoon ground cinnamon
½ cup water
1 cup quick-cooking rolled oats
1 cup packed brown sugar
¼ teaspoon baking powder
¼ teaspoon baking soda
½ cup butter, melted

Place the sliced apples in a 9x13-inch pan. Mix granulated sugar, 1 table-spoon flour, and ground cinnamon together, and sprinkle over apples. Pour water evenly over all; set aside. In a large bowl, combine oats, remaining 1 cup flour, brown sugar, baking powder, baking soda, and melted butter. Stir to combine and then crumble evenly over the apple mixture. Bake at 350 degrees F. for about 45 minutes, or until top is golden brown and apples are tender. Serves 12 to 15.

Quick Swiss Apple Pie

Pastry for 9-inch double-crust pie (see page 8)
1 (21-ounce) can cherry pie filling
1 (21-ounce) can apple pie filling
½ teaspoon ground cinnamon
¼ teaspoon ground nutmeg

Roll out pastry for bottom crust and line pie pan. Roll out top crust. Make 4 to 6 slits with a knife to vent; set aside. Discard ⅓ cup of juice from cherry filling and then spoon remaining juice and cherries into bottom of pie shell. Gently spoon entire can of apple filling over cherries. Sprinkle with cinnamon and nutmeg. Moisten edge of pie crust with water. Add top crust and seal. Brush with milk and sprinkle with sugar. Bake at 375 degrees F. for 35 to 45 minutes. Makes 1 pie.

Quick Swiss Apple Pie

Raisin Apple Pie

Raisin Apple Pie

Pastry for 9-inch double-crust pie (see page 8)
¾ cup raisins
1½ cups plus 2 tablespoons water, divided
½ cup sugar
1 tablespoon lemon juice
¼ teaspoon salt
2 tablespoons butter
¾ teaspoon vanilla
2 tablespoons cornstarch
1½ cups sliced apples (water-packed canned, drained)
¼ cup coarsely chopped walnuts

In a large saucepan, boil raisins and 1½ cups water together for 15 minutes.
Add sugar, lemon juice, salt, butter, and vanilla. Cook until the butter is
melted. In a small bowl, mix together cornstarch and 2 tablespoons water,
then slowly add to the raisin mixture, stirring continuously. Cook until thick.

Mix apples and walnuts together in a separate bowl. Add to the raisin
mixture. Mix together and fill pie. Moisten edge of pie crust with water. Add
top crust and seal. Brush with milk and sprinkle with sugar. Bake at 425
degrees F. for about 50 minutes. Makes 1 pie.

Sugar-Free Apple Pie

Crust

    ½ cup low-fat ricotta cheese
    5 packets artificial sweetener
    3 tablespoons skim milk
    1 egg white
    2 tablespoons vegetable oil
    1½ teaspoons vanilla
    Dash salt
    2 cups flour
    2 teaspoons baking powder
    2 tablespoons water

Filling

    6 medium apples, peeled and sliced
    ¼ cup flour
    ½ teaspoon cinnamon
    12 packets artificial sweetener

For crust: Mix together the ricotta cheese, 5 packets sweetener, milk, egg white, oil, vanilla, and salt. Add 2 cups flour, baking powder, and water and mix until dough forms. Divide pastry into two equal pieces; wrap and place in refrigerator to chill. When ready to use, roll out half of the dough and line a 9-inch pie pan.

For filling: Toss apples with ¼ cup flour, cinnamon, and 12 packets sweetener. Arrange in pie shell. Roll out second half of dough for top crust. Cut two 2-inch slits near center (or make a fancier cutout design, if desired). Moisten the edge of the bottom crust around the rim. Place top crust carefully over pie; trim, leaving ½ inch to extend over rim. Press top and bottom crusts together and flute around rim. Make sure slits are open to allow steam to escape while cooking.

Bake at 375 degrees F. for 20 minutes, then reduce oven temperature to 325 degrees F. and bake 25 minutes longer. Makes 1 pie.

Apricot Pineapple Pie (shown on page 9)

Pastry for 9-inch double-crust pie (see page 8)
1 (15¼-ounce) can apricot halves
1 (20-ounce) can pineapple tidbits
¾ cup sugar
¼ cup plus 2 tablespoons cornstarch
¼ teaspoon salt

Drain and discard ¼ cup apricot juice. Pour apricots and remaining juice into large mixing bowl. Cut apricots in half, making each piece ¼ of an apricot. Drain and discard ½ cup pineapple juice. Add pineapple tidbits and remaining juice to apricots. In separate bowl, mix sugar, cornstarch, and salt; pour on top of fruit. Mix well with rubber spatula.

Fill crust. Moisten edge of pie crust with water. Add top crust and seal. Brush with milk and sprinkle with sugar. Bake at 375 degrees F. for 45 to 50 minutes or until golden brown. Makes 1 pie.

Cheesy Apricot Pie

1 baked 9-inch pie shell or graham cracker crust (see page 10 or 7)
⅓ cup sugar
1 (8-ounce) package cream cheese, softened
1¼ cups cream
1 teaspoon vanilla
¼ teaspoon almond extract
1 (10½-ounce) can apricot halves
1 envelope unflavored gelatin
½ cup currant jelly, melted
Whipped cream, if desired

Beat sugar and cream cheese together until fluffy and light. Beating on low speed, slowly pour in the cream. Blend in vanilla and almond extract.

Drain the apricot halves, reserving the syrup. Place ½ cup of the syrup in a small saucepan; soften the gelatin in the syrup. Slightly heat this mixture to help the gelatin dissolve. Stir gelatin mixture into cream cheese mixture; pour into pie shell and chill 2 to 3 hours, or until set.

Arrange apricot halves on top of the cream filling in a decorative manner. Spoon the melted currant jelly over the apricots. Chill pie. Serve with whipped cream if desired. Makes 1 pie.

Banana Cream Pie

2 baked 9-inch pie shells (see page 10)
4 cups milk, divided
2 cups half-and-half
2 tablespoons butter
1¼ cups granulated sugar, divided
3 egg yolks
¼ teaspoon salt
½ cup cornstarch
1½ teaspoons vanilla
2 large bananas, sliced*
Whipped cream, for garnish

Place 3 cups milk in top pan of a double boiler; add half-and-half, butter, and ¾ cup of the sugar and stir. Heat over medium-high heat until butter is melted and milk is scalded.

In a small bowl, whisk egg yolks well; add remaining ½ cup sugar and salt and whisk very well. Slowly add egg mixture to hot milk mixture, stirring constantly for about half a minute. Allow mixture to cook for 15 to 20 minutes, stirring frequently. (This gives eggs time to cook and start thickening. Undercooking at this point can slow the finishing process by as much as half an hour.)

Mix 1 cup milk and cornstarch in a small bowl and slowly add to hot mixture, stirring constantly to avoid formation of lumps. Continue stirring for at least 2 minutes and then stir every 5 minutes for 15 to 20 minutes. When pudding is thick, stir in vanilla.

Remove double boiler from stove. Before pouring hot filling into pie shells, place sliced bananas into each baked shell. Pour half of the filling into each pie shell, rounding tops of pies. Cool on wire racks and then chill in refrigerator 3 to 4 hours. When ready to serve, whip cream and spread over pies. Makes 2 pies.

*Note: Do not use overripe bananas.

Razanna Cream Pie

2 baked 9-inch pie shells (see page 10)
4 cups milk, divided
2 cups half-and-half
2 tablespoons butter
1¼ cups sugar, divided
3 egg yolks
¼ teaspoon salt
½ cup cornstarch
1½ teaspoons vanilla
2 to 3 bananas, sliced
Raspberry glaze*
Whipped cream, for garnish

Place 3 cups milk in top of a double boiler and add half-and-half, butter, and ¾ cup sugar and stir. Cook until butter is melted and milk looks scalded.

In a bowl, whisk egg yolks until well broken up; then add ½ cup sugar and salt and whisk together very well. Slowly add this mixture to the hot milk mixture, stirring constantly. Stir for approximately ½ minute and then allow to cook for 15 to 20 minutes. (This gives the eggs time to cook and start the thickening process. Undercooking at this point slows the finishing process down by as much as half an hour.)

Mix 1 cup milk and cornstarch together and slowly add to the hot mixture. Be careful to stir constantly or lumps will form. Continue stirring for at least 2 minutes and every 5 minutes for the next 15 to 20 minutes.

When pudding is thick enough, stir in vanilla. Remove the whole double boiler from stove (the hot water will help keep the pudding hot while you assemble the pies).

Slice bananas in bottom of each pie shell. Pour filling on top of bananas, leaving room for raspberry glaze. Cool on wire racks and then chill in refrigerator 3 to 4 hours. Spread raspberry glaze on top of cream filling and serve. Makes 2 pies.

*Note: For raspberry glaze, thin ¾ cup raspberry preserves with 2 tablespoons warm water.

Razanna Cream Pie

Blueberry Pie

Pastry for 9-inch double-crust pie (see page 8)
1 (16-ounce) bag frozen blueberries, thawed
1 cup granulated sugar
¼ teaspoon salt
4 tablespoons cornstarch

Roll out pastry for bottom crust and line pie pan. Roll out pastry for top crust, fold in half, and cut three ½-inch slits through both layers of crust, then set aside. Pour thawed berries and juice into a large mixing bowl. In a separate bowl, mix sugar, salt, and cornstarch; pour on top of berries. Mix well with rubber spatula.

Fill crust. Moisten edge of pie crust with water. Add top crust and seal. Brush with milk and sprinkle with sugar. Bake at 375 degrees F. for 45 to 50 minutes, or until golden brown. Makes 1 pie.

Boysenberry Pie

Pastry for 9-inch double-crust pie (see page 8)
1 (16-ounce) bag frozen boysenberries, thawed
1 cup sugar
¼ teaspoon salt
2½ tablespoons cornstarch

Roll out pastry for bottom crust and line pie pan. Roll out pastry for top crust, fold in half, and cut three ½-inch slits through both layers of crust, then set aside. Pour thawed berries and juice into large mixing bowl. In separate bowl, mix sugar, salt, and cornstarch; pour on top of berries. Mix well with rubber spatula.

Fill crust. Moisten edge of pie crust with water. Add top crust and seal. Brush with milk and sprinkle with sugar. Bake at 375 degrees F. for 45 to 50 minutes or until golden brown. Makes 1 pie.

Cranberry Pecan Pie

Cranberry Pecan Pie

1 unbaked 9-inch pie shell (see page 10)*
3 eggs, slightly beaten
2 cups plus 3 tablespoons sugar
½ teaspoon salt
½ cup plus 1½ tablespoons dark corn syrup
½ teaspoon vanilla
1½ tablespoons butter, melted
1½ cups cranberries, fresh or frozen (not thawed)
¾ cup finely chopped pecans

In a large bowl, slightly beat eggs, then add sugar and whisk together with a wire whisk. Add salt, corn syrup, vanilla, and butter. Mix well.

Place cranberries in bottom of an unbaked 9-inch pie shell. Sprinkle pecans on top of cranberries. Slowly pour filling evenly on top of pecans. Bake at 350 degrees F. for 50 to 60 minutes, or until filling is set. Allow to cool completely before cutting. Makes 1 pie.

Note: Be sure to bake in a 9-inch pie shell; an 8-inch shell will overflow.

Cranberry Pie

1 baked 9-inch pie shell (see page 10)
2½ cups fresh cranberries
1 cup water
¾ cup raisins
1 cup sugar
4 tablespoons cornstarch
½ cup chopped walnuts
2 tablespoons butter
Whipped cream, for garnish

In a medium saucepan, cook cranberries in 1 cup water over medium-high heat until cranberries pop. Add raisins. Combine sugar and cornstarch in a small bowl and stir into cranberry mixture. Cook and stir until mixture thickens and bubbles. Add nuts and butter and stir until butter melts.

Pour into baked pie shell. Cool. Serve topped with a dollop of whipped cream. Makes 1 pie.

Cranberry Pie

Fresh Berry Tart

Fresh Berry Tart

Pastry

> 6 tablespoons sugar
> ⅔ cup margarine
> 1½ tablespoons cream
> 1 egg yolk
> ½ teaspoon almond extract
> 1¼ cups cake flour

Filling

> 3 cups strawberries*, blueberries, blackberries, boysenberries, or Marion
> berries
> 1 (3-ounce) package cream cheese, room temperature
> 4 tablespoons sugar, divided
> ½ (8-ounce) container frozen whipped topping, thawed in the refrigerator

For pastry: Place sugar and margarine in a medium bowl and cream together. Add cream, egg yolk, and almond extract and mix till well blended. Add cake flour and mix until the dough comes together and leaves the sides of the bowl clean. Remove dough from bowl and wrap in plastic wrap. Refrigerate 30 minutes.

Roll dough out until it is 1½ inches larger than 9-inch tart pan. Transfer dough to tart pan gently easing into the bottom and up the sides. Press slightly into the sides of the pan letting the excess hang over the edges. Roll rolling pin over the top edge of the tart pan to seal and cut off the extra dough. Place a piece of aluminum foil that is slightly larger than the tart shell on top of the dough, gently pressing it against the bottom and sides. Pour 1½ cups baking beads, dry beans, or rice on top of the foil (this prevents the dough from rising during baking). Bake at 350 degrees F. for 15 minutes. Remove foil by bringing the corners together and lifting the bundle off. Return crust to the oven and bake for 10 minutes or until golden brown. Allow to cool completely before filling.

For filling: Rinse berries and dry by placing on a double layer of paper towels with another layer on top. Beat cream cheese and 1 tablespoon sugar until smooth. Add whipped topping and mix until well blended. Spread filling in tart shell, arrange berries on top of filling and sprinkle with 3 tablespoons sugar. Makes 1 tart.

Note: Cut strawberries in half or in quarters.

Fresh Strawberry Pie

1 baked 9-inch pie shell (see page 10)
4 cups diced ripe strawberries
2 cups granulated sugar
½ teaspoon salt
½ cup cornstarch
½ teaspoon lemon zest
2 tablespoons freshly squeezed lemon juice
2 cups halved ripe strawberries
½ cup fresh blueberries, divided
Whipped cream, for garnish

Place diced strawberries in a gallon-sized zipper-lock bag; seal well and knead bag to crush berries. Pour crushed berries into a large saucepan and combine with sugar and salt. Remove 1 cup of this mixture and blend with cornstarch in a small bowl; pour back into saucepan. Cook and stir strawberry mixture over medium-high heat until it comes to a boil. Reduce heat to medium and continue to stir and scrape the bottom of the pan until thick and clear. Stir in lemon zest. Place in a chilled, medium-sized bowl and cool in refrigerator, about 1 hour. Stir in lemon juice.

Place halved strawberries and ¼ cup of the blueberries in bottom of baked pie shell. Spoon chilled glaze over berries. Garnish with whipped cream and remaining blueberries. Makes 1 pie.

Fresh Strawberry Pie

Two-Crust Cranberry Pie

Pastry for 9-inch double-crust pie (see page 8)
2 cups raw cranberries
1 cup water
1 cup sugar
1¾ tablespoons cornstarch
¼ to ½ cup chopped walnuts
2 teaspoons butter or margarine

In a medium saucepan, cook cranberries in water until cranberries pop. Strain and save the juice in pan. Mix sugar and cornstarch together and then add to juice. Cook mixture until it thickens and bubbles, stirring constantly. Stir in walnuts, cranberries, and butter.

Pour into pie shell. Moisten edge of pie crust with water. Add top crust and seal. Brush with milk and sprinkle with sugar. Bake at 400 degrees F. for 10 minutes. Reduce heat to 350 degrees F. and bake for 45 minutes more or until crust is nicely browned. Makes 1 pie.

Very Berry Pie (shown on page 26)

Pastry for two 9-inch double-crust pies (see page 8)
1 (16-ounce) bag frozen boysenberries, thawed
1 (8-ounce) bag frozen blueberries, thawed
1 (8-ounce) bag frozen raspberries, thawed
1¾ cups granulated sugar
½ teaspoon salt
½ cup cornstarch

Roll out pastry for 2 bottom crusts and line 2 pie pans. Roll out pastry for 2 top crusts; fold each in half and cut three ½-inch slits through both layers of both crusts, then set aside. Pour thawed berries and all their juices into a large mixing bowl. In a separate bowl, mix sugar, salt, and cornstarch and pour on top of berries. Mix well with rubber spatula.

Fill crusts. Moisten edge of pie crust with water. Add top crust and seal. Brush with milk and sprinkle with sugar. Bake at 375 degrees F. for 45 to 50 minutes, or until golden brown. Makes 2 pies.

Cherry Pie

Cherry Pie

Pastry for 9-inch double-crust pie (see page 8)
2½ tablespoons quick-cooking tapioca
⅛ teaspoon salt
1 cup granulated sugar
3 cups water-packed red sour cherries, drained, with juice reserved
6 drops red food coloring
¼ teaspoon almond extract
1 tablespoon butter

Roll out pastry for bottom crust and line pie pan. Roll out pastry for top crust, fold in half, and cut three ½-inch slits through both layers of crust, then set aside.*

Combine tapioca, salt, and sugar in a large bowl. Measure ½ cup of the reserved cherry juice and add to bowl, along with cherries, food coloring, and almond extract. Mix well. Let stand about 15 minutes and then pour into pie shell; dot with butter.

Unfold top pie crust and place over pie; press top and bottom crusts together around edge. Crimp or flute. Bake at 375 degrees F. for 45 to 50 minutes. Makes 1 pie.

Note: See DVD for demonstration on how to make a lattice pie crust.

Ezra Taft Benson's Lemon Meringue Pie

1 baked 9-inch pie shell (see page 10)
Zest from 2 lemons
3 cups plus 3 tablespoons sugar, divided
2 heaping tablespoons flour
2 heaping tablespoons cornstarch
5 eggs, separated
4 cups water
Juice of 2 lemons
1 tablespoon butter

In a large saucepan, place lemon zest, 3 cups sugar, flour, and cornstarch. Stir in well-beaten egg yolks, then water and lemon juice. Cook over medium heat, stirring constantly until the mixture is thickened. Stir in butter. Pour into baked pie shell.

To make meringue, beat egg whites until foamy; stir in 3 tablespoons sugar and continue beating until stiff. Carefully spoon onto pie. Bake at 425 to 450 degrees F. for 3 to 5 minutes, or until meringue is lightly browned. Makes 1 pie.

Source: Flora Amussen Benson, wife of President Ezra Taft Benson.

Lemon Pie

1 baked 9-inch pie shell (see page 10)
1½ cups sugar
7 tablespoons cornstarch
5 egg yolks
2 cups water
½ cup lemon juice
2 tablespoons butter

In a bowl, mix together sugar and cornstarch; pour mixture in top of a double boiler* not yet on the pan of water.

Place 5 egg yolks in a bowl and whisk until well mixed. Slowly pour ⅛ cup of water into egg yolks while whisking. Pour in remaining water and then pour egg mixture into the double boiler with the sugar mixture. Add lemon juice; stir well.

Place double boiler on top of water pan and cook, stirring well every 6 to 7 minutes for 30 to 40 minutes or until thick and clear. (It is very important to stir often or the cornstarch will make large lumps.) Remove from heat. Cut butter into pieces and add to hot mixture. Stir until butter is melted and well blended. Pour into baked pie shell. Top with meringue or whipped cream. (For instructions on making meringue, see recipe for Ezra Taft Benson's Lemon Meringue Pie on page 58.) Makes 1 pie.

*Note: Pudding may be made in a stainless steel bowl that fits on a pan of water if a double boiler is not available.

Lemon Truffle Pie

1 graham cracker crust or baked 9-inch pie shell (see page 7 or 10)
3 tablespoons cornstarch
⅓ cup sugar plus ¼ cup sugar, divided
1½ cups water
5 tablespoons lemon juice
Zest from 2 lemons
4 egg yolks, beaten
1½ tablespoons butter
1 cup white chocolate chips
2 (8-ounce) packages cream cheese, room temperature
1 cup whipped cream
Toasted sliced almonds, for garnish

Mix cornstarch and ⅓ cup sugar in a medium saucepan; add water and stir. Stir in lemon juice and lemon zest. In a separate bowl beat egg yolks with a fork; add ¼ cup sugar and mix well. Add this mixture to the first and whisk together. Cook on medium heat, stirring constantly until mixture boils for one minute.

Remove from heat; add butter and stir until melted. Remove 1½ cups of liquid and reserve for top layer. Add white chocolate chips to remaining liquid and stir until they are melted and mixed in well. Cut the cream cheese in small cubes and add to the white chocolate mixture. Stir until well mixed and smooth. (You may need to use an electric mixer.)

Pour mixture into a baked 9-inch pie shell or a graham cracker crust. Pour the reserved lemon sauce on top and chill at least 2 hours. Spread whipped cream over lemon filling. Garnish with toasted sliced almonds. Makes 1 pie.

Lemon Truffle Pie

Lemon Chiffon Pie

Crust

1¼ cups graham cracker crumbs
⅓ cup butter, melted
¼ cup sugar

Filling

1 envelope unflavored gelatin
1 cup sugar, divided
⅛ teaspoon salt
4 eggs, separated
½ cup cold water
1 teaspoon lemon zest
½ cup lemon juice
Whipped cream, for topping
Lemon slices, for garnish

For crust: Mix graham cracker crumbs, melted butter, and ¼ cup sugar in a small bowl. Press mixture evenly in bottom and up sides of a 9-inch pie pan. Bake at 375 degrees F. for 8 minutes. Cool on a wire rack.

For filling: Combine gelatin, ½ cup sugar, and salt in a medium saucepan. Stir in well-beaten egg yolks, water, lemon zest, and lemon juice. Cook and stir over medium heat until gelatin dissolves and mixture is thick and bubbly. Remove from heat. Chill to consistency of corn syrup, stirring occasionally.

Beat egg whites until soft peaks form. Gradually add the remaining ½ cup sugar, beating until stiff peaks form. Fold egg whites into lemon mixture. Spoon into graham cracker shell. Chill for several hours before serving. Serve with a dollop of whipped cream and garnish with a thin lemon slice. Makes 1 pie.

Key Lime Pie

2 graham cracker crusts or baked 9-inch pie shells (see page 7 or 10)
2 envelopes (or 2 tablespoons) unflavored gelatin
1¾ cups sugar, divided
¼ teaspoon salt
6 eggs, separated
¾ cup lime juice
½ cup water
1 teaspoon lime zest
Few drops green food coloring
Whipped cream
Lime, thinly sliced for garnish

Mix gelatin, 1 cup sugar, and salt. Beat egg yolks, lime juice, and water; pour into a saucepan. Add gelatin mixture; stir constantly over medium heat until mixture boils. Stir in lime zest and food coloring. Pour into bowl (do not leave in aluminum pan) and refrigerate until mixture mounds when dropped from spoon. Beat egg whites until soft peaks form. Gradually add ¾ cup sugar and continue beating until stiff. Fold into lime mixture.

Pour into pie shells. Serve with whipped cream and garnish with thin slices of lime. Makes 2 pies.

Lime Chiffon Pie

Lime Chiffon Pie

1 baked 9-inch Lite Pie Crust (see page 11)
¼ cup sugar
1 envelope (or 1 tablespoon) unflavored gelatin
½ cup water
¼ cup lime juice
2 egg yolks
1 teaspoon lime zest
1 drop green food coloring, if desired
3 egg whites
¼ cup sugar
1 (8-ounce) frozen whipped topping, thawed

In a medium saucepan, combine ¼ cup sugar and gelatin. Add water and lime juice. Cook and stir over low heat until gelatin is completely dissolved. In a medium bowl slightly beat egg yolks. Gradually stir gelatin mixture into egg yolks and then return all of the egg yolk mixture to the saucepan. Bring to a gentle boil; cook and stir 2 minutes more. Remove from heat. Cool slightly. Stir in lime zest and food coloring. Cover and chill until mixture is the consistency of syrup, stirring occasionally.

In a medium bowl, beat the egg whites with an electric mixer on medium speed until soft peaks form. Gradually add ¼ cup sugar, beating on high speed until stiff peaks form. Fold egg whites into slightly thickened gelatin.

Fold whipped topping into gelatin mixture. If necessary, chill the filling until it mounds when spooned (about 1 hour). Spoon the filling into the baked pie shell. Cover and chill at least 4 hours (or overnight, if desired). Makes 1 pie.

Deep-Dish Peach and Sour Cherry Pie

Pastry for 9-inch double-crust pie (see page 8)

Filling

4 cups sliced fresh peaches
2 cups sour cherries
⅔ cup granulated sugar
1 tablespoon lemon juice
¼ cup packed brown sugar
3 tablespoons cornstarch
¼ teaspoon ground cinnamon

Crumb Topping

1 cup all-purpose flour
½ cup rolled oats
⅔ cup packed brown sugar
½ teaspoon ground cinnamon
½ cup butter cut into ¼-inch pieces

Prepare pastry and roll three-fourths of the dough into a large round. Line a 9-inch deep-dish pie pan with pastry round, trim and flute edges, and set aside.

For filling: In a large bowl, toss peaches and cherries in granulated sugar and lemon juice. Let sit for 10 minutes to allow fruit to release juices. In a small bowl, mix ¼ cup brown sugar, cornstarch, and cinnamon. Add to fruit mixture and toss to coat. Pour filling into pastry and bake at 400 degrees F. for 30 minutes.

For crumb topping: Pulse flour, oats, ⅔ cup brown sugar, and cinnamon in a food processor several times to mix. Scatter the butter pieces over the top and pulse until it resembles small crumbs. Empty the crumbs into a large bowl and rub them between your fingers until you have large buttery crumbs. Refrigerate until ready to use.

Remove the pie from the oven and reduce the temperature to 375 degrees F. Spread the crumbs over the surface of the pie and press down slightly. Return the pie to the oven and continue to bake until the top is brown and the juices bubble thickly at the edge, 35 to 40 minutes. Cool for at least 2 hours before serving. Makes 1 pie.

Note: The unused pie crust can be rolled out, cut into shapes and sprinkled with cinnamon sugar. Bake on a cookie sheet at 400 degrees F. for 8 to 12 minutes.

Fresh Peach Pie

1 baked 9-inch pie shell (see page 10)
3 cups water
1 cup granulated sugar
1 (3-ounce) package peach flavored gelatin
3 tablespoons cornstarch
4 cups sliced peaches
Whipped cream, for garnish

In a medium saucepan, bring water and sugar to a boil over medium-high heat. Mix gelatin and cornstarch together and gradually add to the boiling sugar water. Cook over medium-high heat, stirring constantly for 5 minutes or until mixture is clear and thickened slightly; remove from heat. Let stand at room temperature until cool and thickened like a heavy syrup. (Or refrigerate to cool, stirring often, so it doesn't set up too much.) Pour over fresh peaches and fold together gently.

Mound mixture in baked pie shell. Chill for at least 2 hours before serving. Top each slice with a dollop of whipped cream, if desired. Makes 1 pie.

Peach Pie

Pastry for double-crust pie (see page 8)
1 (29-ounce) can peach slices
½ cup sugar
¼ cup plus 2 tablespoons cornstarch
¼ teaspoon salt
⅛ teaspoon cinnamon

Drain and discard ½ cup juice from peaches. Pour peaches and remaining juice into a large mixing bowl. In a separate bowl, mix together sugar, cornstarch, salt, and cinnamon; pour on top of peaches. Mix well with a rubber spatula.

Fill crust. Moisten edge of pie crust with water. Add top crust and seal. Brush with milk and sprinkle with sugar. Bake at 375 degrees F. for 45 to 50 minutes or until golden brown. Makes 1 pie.

Pear and Cherry Crisp

1 (16-ounce) package frozen unsweetened pitted tart red cherries, thawed
    and drained (set juice aside), or 1 (16-ounce) can pitted tart red cherries
    (water-packed)
⅓ to ½ cup granulated sugar
2 tablespoons all-purpose flour
1 teaspoon orange zest
½ teaspoon ground cinnamon
3 to 4 medium pears, peeled, cored, and thinly sliced (3 cups total)*
½ cup granola or streusel
2 tablespoons butter, melted
Vanilla ice cream (optional)

If using canned cherries, drain cherries, reserving ½ cup of the juice. In a
large mixing bowl, combine frozen or canned cherries and reserved juice;
add sugar and toss to coat. Let stand for 5 minutes.

In a small bowl, combine flour, orange zest, and cinnamon. Sprinkle over
cherries and toss to mix. Add sliced pears and toss to mix. Transfer mixture
to an ungreased 2-quart square baking dish. Combine granola and butter
and sprinkle over filling. Bake at 375 degrees F. about 30 minutes, or until
pears are tender. If necessary, to prevent overbrowning, cover with foil the
last 5 to 10 minutes. Serve warm with ice cream. Serves 8.

Note: Canned, sliced pears may be used in place of fresh pears, if desired.

Pear Crisp Pie

1 recipe Oatmeal Crisp Pie Crust (see page 12)
8 cups peeled, cored, and sliced pears (½-inch thick or thicker)
¾ cup granulated sugar
1 tablespoon lemon juice
3 tablespoons cornstarch
2 to 3 tablespoons chopped crystallized ginger
1 teaspoon ground cinnamon
½ teaspoon freshly grated nutmeg

Line 2 pie pans with Oatmeal Crisp Pie Crust and set aside.

In a large bowl, combine pears, sugar, lemon juice, cornstarch, ginger, cinnamon, and nutmeg. Toss well.

Pour half of mixture into each unbaked pie shell. Cover both pies with vented pastry tops. Moisten edge of pie crust with water. Add top crust and seal. Brush tops with milk and sprinkle with sugar, if desired.

Bake at 400 degrees F. for 1 hour, or until top crusts are golden brown. Makes 2 pies.

Quick Mincemeat Pie

Filling

Pastry for two 9-inch double-crust pies (see page 8)
1 (27-ounce) jar mincemeat
1 (21-ounce) can apple pie filling (cut apples in smaller pieces)
¾ cup nuts, chopped

Holiday Sauce

½ cup granulated sugar
½ cup brown sugar
2 tablespoons cornstarch
Pinch salt
1 cup water
1 tablespoon butter
½ teaspoon imitation rum flavoring

For filling: Pour all filling ingredients into medium bowl and stir. Line two 9-inch pie pans with dough. Divide filling evenly. Moisten edge of pie crusts with water. Add top crusts and seal. Brush with milk and sprinkle with sugar. Bake at 375 degrees F. for 45 to 50 minutes. Makes 2 pies.

For holiday sauce: Mix sugars, cornstarch, and salt in a small saucepan until well blended. Add water and bring to a boil, stirring constantly. Add butter and imitation rum flavoring. Makes about 1½ cups.

Serve mincemeat pie with warm Holiday Sauce.

Raisin Cream Pie

Pastry for 9-inch double-crust pie (see page 8)
1 cup seedless raisins
1½ cups water
¾ cup sugar
3 tablespoons cornstarch
¼ teaspoon salt
1 teaspoon vanilla
1 tablespoon butter
1 cup light cream

Rinse and drain raisins, then place in a large saucepan; add water, and boil slowly over medium heat for 10 minutes. Blend sugar, cornstarch, and salt in a small bowl and add to raisin mixture. Cook over medium heat, stirring constantly, until mixture is clear and thick. Remove from heat and stir in vanilla, butter, and cream. Allow to cool completely.

Pour into pastry-lined pie pan. Moisten edge of pie crust with water. Add top crust and seal. Brush with milk and sprinkle with sugar. Bake at 400 degrees F. for 30 minutes, or until pastry is light brown. Serve warm or cold. Makes 1 pie.

Raisin Pie

Pastry for 9-inch double-crust pie, rolled thin (see page 8)
1½ cups raisins
1½ cups water
¼ cup pineapple juice, or ¼ cup more water
½ teaspoon vanilla
1 cup sugar
¼ cup cornstarch
½ teaspoon salt
¼ cup lemon juice

In small saucepan, combine raisins, water, pineapple juice, and vanilla. Bring to a boil and cook 5 minutes. Pour mixture through strainer. Set raisins aside, reserving liquid.

Mix sugar, cornstarch, and salt; add hot raisin liquid, beating with wire whip. Continue cooking and stirring until thick, about 5 minutes. Add raisins and lemon juice; pour into unbaked pie shell.

Roll out top crust and cut two 2-inch slits near center, then snip with scissors at sides and between slits, or make cutout designs. Moisten edge of bottom crust with water. To adjust top crust, fold in half or roll loosely on rolling pin; center on filling. Pull slits apart slightly if necessary with knife, for steam to escape during baking. Trim top crust, allowing it to extend half an inch over rim. To seal, press top and bottom crusts together around rim.

Fold edge of top crust under bottom crust; flute. Bake at 375 degrees F. for about 50 minutes or to the desired brownness. Makes 1 pie.

Rhubarb Pie

Pastry for 9-inch unbaked double-crust pie (see page 8)
4 cups rhubarb (frozen, partially thawed)*
1¾ cups sugar
¼ cup flour
2 tablespoons cornstarch
¼ teaspoon salt
1 egg
1 drop red food coloring

Place rhubarb in medium mixing bowl; let thaw 10 to 15 minutes. Drain liquid. In separate bowl, combine sugar, flour, cornstarch, and salt. Beat egg; blend with flour mixture. Add rhubarb and red food coloring; mix well.

Pour into unbaked pie shell. Roll out top crust; cut slits and place over filling. Seal; flute edges. Brush top with milk; sprinkle with sugar, if desired. Bake at 350 degrees F. for 45 minutes or until browned. Makes 1 pie.

Note: Four cups fresh rhubarb may be substituted for frozen rhubarb. Bake at 350 degrees F. for 50 to 55 minutes.

Almond Coconut Pie

2 9-inch chocolate ready crusts (purchase pre-made at your local store)
4 cups milk, divided
2 cups half-and-half
2 tablespoons butter
1¼ cups sugar, divided
3 egg yolks
¼ teaspoon salt
½ cup cornstarch
1½ teaspoons vanilla
1⅔ cups coconut, divided
1⅔ cups almonds, slivered and toasted, divided
1½ cups grated chocolate, divided
Whipped cream, for garnish

Place 3 cups milk in top of a double boiler and add half-and-half, butter, and ¾ cup sugar and stir. Cook until butter is melted and milk looks scalded.

In a bowl, whisk egg yolks until well broken up; then add ½ cup sugar and salt and whisk together very well. Slowly add this mixture to the hot milk mixture, stirring constantly. Stir for approximately ½ minute and then allow to cook for 15 to 20 minutes. (This gives the eggs time to cook and start the thickening process. Undercooking at this point slows the finishing process down by as much as half an hour.)

Mix 1 cup milk and cornstarch together and slowly add to the hot mixture. Be careful to stir constantly or lumps will form. Continue stirring for at least 2 minutes and every 5 minutes for the next 15 to 20 minutes.

When pudding is thick enough, stir in vanilla. Stir in ⅔ cup coconut and ⅔ cup almonds. Remove the whole double boiler from stove (the hot water will help keep the pudding hot while you assemble the pies).

Place ½ cup grated chocolate into bottom of pie shells. Pour filling over chocolate in pie shells. Fill pies so the tops are a little rounded. Cool at least 2 hours. Top with whipped cream and garnish with remaining chocolate, coconut, and almonds. Makes 2 pies.

Coconut Cream Pie

2 baked 9-inch pie shells (see page 10)
4 cups milk, divided
2 cups half-and-half
2 tablespoons butter
1¼ cups granulated sugar, divided
3 egg yolks
¼ teaspoon salt
½ cup cornstarch
1½ teaspoons vanilla
1¼ cups coconut, divided (toasted, if desired)
Whipped cream, for garnish

Place 3 cups milk in top pan of a double boiler; add half-and-half, butter, and ¾ cup of the sugar and stir. Heat over medium-high heat until butter is melted and milk is scalded.

In a small bowl, whisk egg yolks well; add remaining ½ cup sugar and salt and whisk very well. Slowly add egg mixture to hot milk mixture, stirring constantly for about half a minute; allow mixture to cook for 15 to 20 minutes, stirring frequently. (This gives eggs time to cook and start thickening. Undercooking at this point can slow the finishing process by as much as half an hour.)

Mix 1 cup milk and cornstarch in a small bowl and slowly add to hot mixture, stirring constantly to avoid formation of lumps. Continue stirring for at least 2 minutes and then stir every 5 minutes for 15 to 20 minutes. When pudding is thick, stir in vanilla and 1 cup coconut. Remove double boiler from stove. Pour half of the filling into each pie shell, rounding tops of pies. Cool on wire racks then chill in refrigerator 3 to 4 hours. When ready to serve, whip cream and spread over pie. Top each pie with another ¼ cup coconut. Makes 2 pies.

Coconut Cream Pie

Pineapple Cream Pie

Crust

¾ cup butter
1½ cups flour
½ cup chopped nuts

Pineapple Filling

1 (20-ounce) can crushed pineapple in juice, divided
⅓ cup cornstarch
4 egg yolks
1 tablespoon water
1 cup sugar
¼ teaspoon salt
2 cups whole milk
2 tablespoons butter or
   margarine
1 teaspoon vanilla

Cream Cheese Filling

1 (8-ounce) package cream
   cheese, softened
½ cup powdered sugar
½ teaspoon vanilla
⅓ cup finely chopped macadamia
   nuts
⅓ cup reserved drained pineapple

Topping

1 cup whipping cream
¼ cup powdered sugar
Remaining pineapple, liquid
   squeezed out
Chopped macadamia nuts

For crust: Mix together butter, flour, and nuts in a medium bowl. Press into a 9x13-inch pan. Bake at 375 degrees F. for 15 minutes or until golden brown. Cool completely.

For pineapple filling: Measure 1 cup pineapple and juice, reserving remaining pineapple. Drain juice from measured pineapple. Combine cornstarch, egg yolks, and water in a small bowl. Combine sugar, salt, milk, and drained pineapple in saucepan. Cook over medium heat, stirring constantly, until mixture comes almost to a boil. Reduce heat to low. Add egg yolk mixture slowly, stirring constantly; continue to cook and stir until thickened. Add butter or margarine and vanilla. Remove from heat, cover with wax paper, and refrigerate for 30 minutes, stirring once or twice.

For cream cheese filling: Combine cream cheese and powdered sugar in a medium bowl. Beat with a fork until blended and smooth. Add vanilla, nuts, and ⅓ cup drained pineapple. Mix well. Spread over cooled crust. Top with pineapple filling.

For topping: In a small bowl, whip cream with powdered sugar until soft peaks form. Spread over pie and garnish with pineapple and nuts. (Make sure pineapple is well drained before placing on top of whipped cream.) Serve or refrigerate until ready to serve. Makes 15 servings.

Pineapple Pie

Pastry for 9-inch double-crust pie (see page 8)
2 (20-ounce) cans pineapple tidbits in juice
1 cup sugar
3 tablespoons cornstarch
¼ teaspoon salt
1 drop yellow food coloring

Pour pineapple into a bowl. Discard ¾ cup of the juice; keep the rest. Mix sugar, cornstarch, and salt together in a bowl; pour on top of pineapple. Mix well with a rubber spatula. Add food coloring and mix well.

Fill crust. Moisten edge of pie crust with water. Add top crust and seal. Brush with milk and sprinkle with sugar. Bake at 375 degrees F. for 45 to 50 minutes or until golden brown. Makes 1 pie.

Tropical Isle Pie

2 baked 9-inch pie shells (see page 10)
4 cups milk, divided
2 cups half-and-half
2 tablespoons butter
1¼ cups granulated sugar, divided
3 egg yolks
¼ teaspoon salt
½ cup cornstarch
1½ teaspoons vanilla
1 cup coconut
⅔ cup drained crushed pineapple
⅔ cup drained mandarin oranges
Whipped cream, for garnish

Place 3 cups milk in top pan of a double boiler; add half-and-half, butter, and ¾ cup of the sugar and stir. Heat over medium-high heat until butter is melted and milk is scalded.

In a small bowl, whisk egg yolks well; add remaining ½ cup sugar and salt and whisk very well. Slowly add egg mixture to hot milk mixture, stirring constantly for about half a minute; allow mixture to cook for 15 to 20 minutes, stirring frequently. (This gives eggs time to cook and start thickening. Undercooking at this point can slow the finishing process by as much as half an hour.)

Mix 1 cup milk and cornstarch in a small bowl and slowly add to hot mixture, stirring constantly to avoid formation of lumps. Continue stirring for at least 2 minutes and then stir every 5 minutes for 15 to 20 minutes. When pudding is thick, stir in vanilla, coconut, pineapple, and oranges. Remove double boiler from stove.

Pour half of the filling into each pie shell, rounding tops of pies. Cool on wire racks then chill in refrigerator 2 to 3 hours. Top with whipped cream when ready to serve. Makes 2 pies.

Tropical Isle Pie

Pralines and Cream Pie (see page 93)

Nut Pies and Tarts

Caramel Chocolate Pecan Pie

1 unbaked 9-inch pie shell (see page 10)
1 cup pecan pieces
1 cup semisweet chocolate chips
½ cup caramel ice cream topping
1 (8-ounce) package cream cheese
1 cup dairy sour cream
½ cup sugar
1 teaspoon vanilla
3 eggs
Cocoa powder, for garnish

In the unbaked pie shell, sprinkle the pecan pieces and chocolate chips. Drizzle the caramel topping over the top; set aside while you make the filling.

In a medium bowl, beat the cream cheese until soft. Add the sour cream, sugar, and vanilla and mix until smooth. Add the eggs, beating on low speed until just combined. Pour into the prepared crust. Bake at 350 degrees F. approximately 45 minutes, until the center appears set. Cool and then chill at least 1 hour. Dust with cocoa powder. Makes 1 pie.

Lemon Almond Tart

Pastry

1¾ cups flour
⅓ cup sugar
Pinch of salt
½ cup unsalted butter, softened
1 teaspoon finely grated lemon zest
3 egg yolks
2 tablespoons water

Filling

1½ cups ricotta cheese
½ cup sugar
3 eggs, well beaten
1 tablespoon finely grated lemon zest
¾ cup finely chopped blanched almonds
3 tablespoons sliced almonds
Powdered sugar, for garnish

For pastry: In a large bowl, combine the flour, sugar, and salt. Stir to combine. Make a well in the center and add the butter, zest, egg yolks, and water. Work the flour into the center with a fork or your fingers until a smooth dough forms. Wrap in plastic wrap, flatten slightly, and then refrigerate for 20 minutes. (If it gets too cold you will need to let it warm a little to make it easier to roll out.) Make filling while dough is chilling.

For filling: Place ricotta and sugar in a medium bowl and mix together with electric mixer. Add eggs gradually, beating well after each addition. Add the zest, beating briefly to combine. Stir in chopped almonds. Set aside.

Brush an 8-inch fluted tart pan with melted butter. Roll out the pastry on a lightly floured surface and line the pan, trimming away the extra pastry. Pour the filling in the pastry and smooth the top. Sprinkle with sliced almonds and bake at 350 degrees F. for 55 to 60 minutes or until lightly golden and set.

Cool to room temperature, and then carefully remove the sides from the pan. Lightly dust with powdered sugar and serve at room temperature or chilled. Makes one 8-inch tart.

Linzer Tart

⅔ cup hazelnuts
1¼ cups all-purpose flour, divided
⅓ cup packed brown sugar
6 tablespoons butter, slightly softened
1 large egg
½ teaspoon vanilla
¼ teaspoon cinnamon
¼ teaspoon salt
¼ teaspoon baking powder
¾ cup seedless raspberry jam
Powdered sugar, for garnish

Place hazelnuts in a 9x9-inch metal baking pan. Bake at 350 degrees F. for 15 minutes or until toasted. Wrap hot hazelnuts in a clean cloth towel; roll nuts back and forth to remove most of the skins. Cool completely.

Place half of the nuts and ¼ cup of the flour in a food processor or blender; pulse until nuts are finely ground. Repeat with remaining nuts and ¼ cup of the flour.

Place brown sugar and butter in large bowl. Mix with an electric mixer on low speed until blended. Increase speed to medium high and beat until creamy. Beat in egg and vanilla until smooth. On low speed, beat in ground nut mixture, cinnamon, salt, baking powder, and remaining ¾ cup flour. Mix until just combined.

With floured hands, press two-thirds of dough into bottom and up the side of a 9-inch tart pan with a removable bottom. Wrap tart shell and remaining dough in plastic wrap and refrigerate 30 minutes or until firm.

Spread raspberry jam over bottom of tart shell. Divide remaining dough into 10 equal pieces. On lightly floured surface, with floured hands, roll each piece into an 8½-inch rope. Place 5 ropes, about 1½ inches apart, over the filling; do not seal ends. Starting from the other side, place remaining ropes about 1½ inches apart. (It will look like a lattice, but it isn't as hard to make.) You should have square openings across the jam. Trim ends of ropes even with edge of tart; press ends to seal. With any remaining trimmings, make rope for tart shell and press around inside edge of tart.

Bake at 375 degrees F. for 35 to 40 minutes, or until filling is hot and bubbly and crust is lightly browned. Cool on wire rack at least 1 hour. Sprinkle tart with powdered sugar, if desired. When cool, carefully remove side of pan. Serves 8 to 10.

Mini Pecan Pies

Pastry for double-crust pie (see page 8)
2/3 cup chopped pecans, divided
1 cup packed brown sugar
2/3 cup light corn syrup
2 teaspoons vanilla
3/4 teaspoon salt
2 eggs
2 egg whites
Whipped cream, for garnish
24 pecan halves, for garnish

Coat muffin tins for 24 muffins with nonstick cooking spray. Roll out pastry dough into a large rectangle. Use a round cookie cutter to cut out large circles. Press a dough circle into each muffin cup, lining the sides and bottom with dough. Divide 1/3 cup pecans among the pastry-lined muffin cups; set aside.

In a large bowl, stir remaining 1/3 cup pecans, brown sugar, corn syrup, vanilla, salt, eggs, and egg whites until well combined. Spoon filling into muffin tins. Bake at 375 degrees F. for 20 minutes. Cool in pan 10 minutes and then run knife around the pie crust to loosen. Carefully remove to cooling racks. Serve with a dollop of whipped cream and garnish with a pecan half. Makes 24 mini pies.

Mini Pecan Pies

Peanut Butter Pie

Peanut Butter Pie

2 baked 9-inch pie shells (see page 10)
¾ cup peanut butter
1½ cups powdered sugar
4 cups milk, divided
2 cups half-and-half
2 tablespoons butter
1¼ cups sugar, divided
3 egg yolks
¼ teaspoon salt
½ cup cornstarch
1½ teaspoons vanilla

In a medium bowl, mix together peanut butter and powdered sugar by hand. (This works best using the same technique as for cutting shortening into flour for pie dough.) Put a thin layer of peanut butter mixture in bottom of baked pie shells. Reserve some for garnishing tops of finished pies.

Place 3 cups milk in top of a double boiler and add half-and-half, butter, and ¾ cup sugar and stir. Cook until butter is melted and milk looks scalded.

In a bowl, whisk the egg yolks until well broken up; then add ½ cup sugar and salt and whisk together very well. Slowly add this mixture to the hot milk mixture, stirring constantly. Stir for approximately ½ minute and then allow to cook for 15 to 20 minutes. (This gives the eggs time to cook and start the thickening process. Undercooking at this point slows the finishing process down by as much as half an hour.)

Mix 1 cup milk and cornstarch together and slowly add to the hot mixture. Be careful to stir constantly or lumps will form. Continue stirring for at least 2 minutes and every 5 minutes for the next 15 to 20 minutes. When pudding is thick enough, stir in vanilla. Remove the whole double boiler from stove (the hot water will help keep the pudding hot while you assemble the pies).

Pour filling over peanut butter mixture in pie shells. Fill pies so the tops are a little rounded. Sprinkle reserved peanut butter filling on top. Gently pat the mixture so it doesn't fall off when serving. Chill well. Makes 2 pies.

Pecan Pie

1 unbaked 9-inch pie shell (see page 10)*
3 eggs, slightly beaten
2 cups plus 3 tablespoons sugar
½ teaspoon salt
½ cup plus 1½ tablespoons dark corn syrup
½ teaspoon vanilla
1½ tablespoons butter, melted
1½ cups chopped pecans

In a large bowl, slightly beat eggs and then add sugar and whisk together with a wire whisk. Add salt, corn syrup, vanilla, and butter. Mix well.

Arrange pecans in bottom of pie shell. Pour filling evenly on top of pecans and bake at 350 degrees F. for 50 to 60 minutes or until the filling is set. Allow to cool completely before cutting.

For easiest cutting, refrigerate until pie is completely cold. Carefully turn pie upside down and lay it on a cutting board. Use a knife that is as long as the pie is wide. Press the knife straight down through the pie to make the desired sizes. Carefully lift each piece of pie, turn it over, and place on a plate. Makes 1 pie.

*Note: Be sure to bake in a 9-inch pie shell; an 8-inch shell will overflow.

Pralines and Cream Pie (shown on page 82)

2 baked 9-inch pie shells (see page 10)
4 cups milk, divided
2 cups half-and-half
2 tablespoons butter
1¼ cups granulated sugar, divided
3 egg yolks
¼ teaspoon salt
½ cup cornstarch
1½ teaspoons vanilla
1 cup caramel ice cream topping
1 cup chopped pecans
Whipped cream, for garnish

Place 3 cups milk in top pan of a double boiler; add half-and-half, butter, and ¾ cup sugar and stir. Heat over medium-high heat until butter is melted and milk is scalded.

In a small bowl, whisk egg yolks well; add remaining ½ cup sugar and salt and whisk very well. Slowly add egg mixture to hot milk mixture, stirring constantly for about half a minute; allow mixture to cook for 15 to 20 minutes, stirring frequently. (This gives eggs time to cook and start thickening. Undercooking at this point can slow the finishing process by as much as half an hour.)

Mix 1 cup milk and cornstarch in a small bowl and slowly add to hot mixture, stirring constantly to avoid formation of lumps. Continue stirring for at least 2 minutes and then stir every 5 minutes for 15 to 20 minutes. When pudding is thick, stir in vanilla, caramel topping, and pecans. Remove double boiler from stove. Pour half of the filling into each pie shell, rounding tops of pies. Cool on wire racks then chill in refrigerator 3 to 4 hours. Top with sweetened whipped cream before serving. Makes 2 pies.

White Chocolate Macadamia Pie

1 baked 9-inch pie shell (see page 10)

Filling

1 (8-ounce) package cream cheese, softened
⅓ cup granulated sugar
⅓ cup heavy cream, plus ¾ cup whipped soft
6½ ounces white baking chocolate, melted
½ teaspoon orange zest
⅔ cup chopped macadamia nuts, roasted

Ganache

¾ cup semisweet chocolate chips
½ cup heavy cream

Topping

3 cups sweetened whipped cream
1 to 2 tablespoons chopped macadamia nuts

For filling: Beat cream cheese and sugar with an electric mixer until smooth. Scrape bowl with a spatula and mix in ⅓ cup heavy cream. Add melted white chocolate, orange zest, and nuts and stir just until incorporated. Fold in the whipped cream. Spread into baked pie shell and level off with a rubber spatula. Freeze until solid, about 4 hours.

For ganache: Prepare thirty minutes to an hour before serving. Place chocolate chips in a metal mixing bowl and set aside. Bring cream to a simmer over medium heat. Pour simmering cream over chocolate chips and stir until melted. Set aside and allow to cool slightly. Spread warm ganache over top of the frozen pie, smoothing to the edges with a spatula.

For topping: Place sweetened whipped cream in a piping bag and pipe edges of pie with whipped cream or pipe rosettes onto each piece. Sprinkle with macadamia nuts. Refrigerate until ready to serve. Makes 1 pie.

Note: If desired, you can prepare ganache ahead of time, then reheat before finishing pie. To reheat, place the ganache in the microwave on low power for no more than 10 seconds at a time. Stir after each warming, until ganache pours loosely but is not close to boiling. Be very careful when warming chocolate, as it will burn very quickly when heated in the microwave. Once chocolate is scorched it is unusable.

White Chocolate Macadamia Pie

Pumpkin Cream Cheese Pie (see page 100)

Chapter 5

Pumpkin Pies

Hurray for the Pumpkin Pie

1 unbaked 10-inch pie shell (see page 10)

First Layer

⅔ cup milk chocolate chips
1 cup granulated sugar
2 tablespoons butter or margarine
½ cup light corn syrup
¾ teaspoon vanilla
½ cup evaporated milk
¾ cup chopped macadamia nuts

Second Layer

1 (8-ounce) package cream cheese, softened
¼ cup granulated sugar
½ teaspoon vanilla
1 egg, beaten

Third Layer

1 (15-ounce) can pumpkin
1½ cups melted vanilla ice cream
3 eggs, beaten
⅓ cup packed brown sugar
⅓ cup granulated sugar
½ teaspoon ground ginger
¼ teaspoon salt
1¼ teaspoons ground cinnamon
½ teaspoon nutmeg
¼ teaspoon ground cloves

Topping

½ cup whipping cream
1 tablespoon powdered sugar
1 (8-ounce) package cream cheese, softened
1 cup sugar
¼ cup milk chocolate chips
1 tablespoon margarine or butter
⅓ cup crushed macadamia nuts

Line pie pan with pastry; trim and flute edges. Set aside while preparing first layer.

For first layer: Place milk chocolate chips in a small bowl and set aside. In a heavy saucepan, over medium heat, cook the sugar, butter or margarine, corn syrup, evaporated milk, and vanilla. Bring to a boil and stir continuously for 6 minutes. Remove from heat. Pour $\frac{1}{3}$ cup plus 1 tablespoon of this hot caramel mixture over chocolate chips. Stir until smooth. Pour into bottom of pastry-lined pie pan; pat down with back of spoon. Stir macadamia nuts into remaining caramel mixture and allow to cool slightly before spreading over the chocolate.

For second layer: Beat cream cheese with an electric mixer on medium speed until smooth. Beat in sugar. Add vanilla and the beaten egg and beat until light and smooth. Chill for 20 minutes and then spread over first layer.

For third layer: Combine pumpkin, melted ice cream, beaten eggs, brown sugar, sugar, ginger, salt, cinnamon, nutmeg, and ground cloves in a medium bowl and mix thoroughly. Pour over second layer. Bake at 450 degrees F. for 15 minutes. Reduce heat to 350 degrees F. and bake 50 minutes. Remove from oven and cool on a wire rack.

For topping: Once pie has cooled, beat together whipping cream and powdered sugar until stiff and then set aside. In another bowl, cream the cream cheese and sugar until smooth and fluffy. Fold in the whipped cream. With a cookie scoop, dollop topping around edges.

Melt the chocolate chips with butter or margarine in the microwave on high power in 30-second increments, stirring after each time, until mixture is melted. Cool slightly and then drizzle chocolate over the pie and whipped topping. Sprinkle with crushed macadamia nuts. Makes 1 pie.

Pumpkin Cream Cheese Pie (shown on page 96)

1 unbaked 9-inch pie shell (see page 10)
1 (8-ounce) package cream cheese, softened
¾ cup granulated sugar
½ teaspoon salt
1 teaspoon ground cinnamon
½ teaspoon nutmeg, plus more for garnish
½ teaspoon ground cloves
½ teaspoon ground ginger
2 eggs
1 (15-ounce) can pumpkin
1 teaspoon vanilla
½ cup pecan halves, for garnish
Whipped cream, for garnish

In a large bowl, beat cream cheese, sugar, salt, and spices until fluffy. Add eggs, one at a time, beating well after each. Beat in pumpkin and vanilla. Pour into pie shell. Bake at 350 degrees F. for 55 minutes, or until knife inserted near center comes out clean. During last 15 minutes of baking, place pecan halves around edges for garnish.

Cool on a wire rack and then chill in the refrigerator for 3 to 4 hours. Serve with a dollop of whipped cream and a sprinkle of ground nutmeg. Makes 1 pie.

Pumpkin Pie

1 unbaked 9-inch pie shell (see page 10)
1½ cups canned pumpkin
½ teaspoon ground cinnamon
½ teaspoon nutmeg
¼ teaspoon ground ginger
¼ teaspoon allspice
½ cup granulated sugar
⅓ cup packed brown sugar
1 teaspoon salt
1½ tablespoons cornstarch
2 eggs
1 cup evaporated milk
1 cup water
Whipped cream, for garnish

Place pumpkin in a large mixing bowl. In a separate bowl, mix cinnamon, nutmeg, ginger, allspice, granulated sugar, brown sugar, salt, and corn-starch. Add to pumpkin and mix until blended. Add eggs and evaporated milk and mix until blended. Add water and mix well. Pour into unbaked pie shell and bake at 375 degrees F. for 50 to 60 minutes, or until knife inserted near center comes out clean.

Cool on a wire rack. Top with whipped cream before serving. Makes 1 pie.

Pumpkin Praline Pie

1 unbaked 9-inch pie shell in deep-dish pie pan (see page 10)
½ cup brown sugar
½ cup butter, softened
⅓ cup finely chopped pecans
1½ cups canned pumpkin
½ teaspoon ground cinnamon
½ teaspoon ground nutmeg
¼ teaspoon ginger
¼ teaspoon allspice
½ cup granulated sugar
⅓ cup packed brown sugar
1 teaspoon salt
1½ tablespoons cornstarch
2 eggs
1 cup evaporated milk
1 cup water
Whipped cream, for garnish

Place brown sugar and butter in a small bowl and beat until creamy. Stir in pecans by hand. Spread on the bottom of unbaked pie shell. Set aside.

Place pumpkin in a large mixing bowl. In a separate bowl, mix cinnamon, nutmeg, ginger, allspice, granulated sugar, brown sugar, salt, and cornstarch. Add to pumpkin and mix until blended. Add eggs and evaporated milk and mix until blended. Add water and mix well. Pour over the first mixture.

Bake at 375 degrees F. for 50 to 60 minutes, or until knife inserted near the center comes out clean. Cool on a wire rack. Serve with whipped cream. Makes 1 pie.

Rich Pumpkin Pie

1 unbaked 9-inch pie shell (see page 10)
1 (15-ounce) can pumpkin
2 tablespoons flour
½ teaspoon cinnamon
Pinch nutmeg
Pinch ginger
Pinch cloves
½ teaspoon salt
½ cup brown sugar
2 eggs
2 tablespoons corn syrup
1 cup milk
½ cup evaporated milk

Put pumpkin, flour, cinnamon, nutmeg, ginger, cloves, salt, and brown sugar in a large bowl. Blend together. Slowly add eggs, corn syrup, milk, and evaporated milk. Mix well.

Pour into unbaked pie shell. Let sit 60 minutes and then bake at 375 degrees F. for 60 minutes or until a knife inserted in the center comes out clean. Makes 1 pie.

Baked Alaska Pie (see page 106)

Chapter 6

Smooth and Creamy Pies

Baked Alaska Pie (shown on page 104)

1 baked 9-inch pie shell (see page 10)
1 quart peppermint ice cream, slightly softened
2 to 3 tablespoons chocolate syrup
5 egg whites
1 teaspoon vanilla
½ teaspoon cream of tartar
⅔ cup sugar

Spoon ice cream into baked pie shell. Drizzle with chocolate syrup. Place in freezer until ready to use.

With an electric mixer, beat egg whites, vanilla, and cream of tartar until foamy. Gradually beat in sugar until mixture is stiff and glossy. Completely cover ice cream in pie shell with meringue, sealing well to edge of crust and piling high. (If desired, pie may be frozen up to 24 hours at this point.)

When ready to serve, bake pie at 500 degrees F. on lowest oven rack for 3 to 5 minutes, or until meringue is light brown. Serve immediately, or return to freezer until ready to serve. Makes 1 pie.

Buttermilk Pie

1½ cups sugar
1 cup buttermilk
½ cup Bisquick
⅓ cup margarine or butter, melted
1 teaspoon vanilla
3 eggs
Fresh fruit, for garnish
Caramel sauce, for garnish (see page 30)
Whipped cream, for garnish

Grease pie pan. Mix all ingredients and pour into pie pan. Bake at 350 degrees F. for about 30 minutes, or until knife inserted in center comes out clean. Cool 5 minutes. Serve warm or cold with fresh fruit or caramel sauce and whipped cream.

Butterscotch Cream Pie

1 baked 9-inch pie shell (page 10)
1⅓ cups sugar
2½ cups milk
¾ cup whipped cream
5 tablespoons cornstarch
3 egg yolks*
¼ teaspoon salt
1 teaspoon vanilla
2 tablespoons butter or margarine
1 cup whipping cream
¼ cup chopped nuts or toasted coconut, for garnish

Measure sugar into a heavy saucepan or skillet. Stir constantly over high heat until sugar is nearly melted. Reduce heat to medium and continue stirring until all sugar is melted and a light amber color. In the meantime, heat milk. Stir hot milk into melted sugar cautiously. Sugar will bubble and steam, then harden. Keep heat on low and stir occasionally until the hard sugar completely dissolves in the milk.

In a small bowl, add whipped cream to cornstarch gradually to make a smooth paste and then stir into hot milk mixture. Cook and stir until a smooth, thick pudding is formed. Let it boil a minute or two, stirring vigorously, then remove from heat. Place egg yolks in a small bowl and beat with a fork. Add salt, and then stir in some of the hot pudding. Stir egg mixture back into pudding and cook another 2 or 3 minutes. Remove from heat. Add vanilla and butter. Cool 5 minutes and then pour into baked pie shell. Chill 3 to 4 hours.

When ready to serve, whip the cream and spread over pie. Sprinkle with nuts or toasted coconut. Makes 1 pie.

Note: 2 whole eggs may be used, but filling may not be as smooth.

Butterscotch Cream Pie

Joseph F. Smith's Custard Pie

1 unbaked 9-inch pie shell (see page 10)
2 cups milk
4 eggs
½ cup sugar
Pinch salt
Generous sprinkling nutmeg

Put milk in a medium bowl. Beat eggs and strain through fine sieve into bowl of milk. Add sugar, salt, and nutmeg. Stir well and pour into pie shell. Bake at 375 degrees F. until knife inserted in the center just barely comes out clean, about 50 to 60 minutes. Do not overcook, or custard will become watery. Makes 1 pie.

Note: This recipe does not call for vanilla.

Source: Salt Lake City 18th Ward Cookbook.

Vanilla Cream Pie

2 baked 9-inch pie shells (see page 10)
4 cups milk, divided
2 cups half-and-half
2 tablespoons butter
1¼ cups sugar, divided
3 egg yolks
¼ teaspoon salt
½ cup cornstarch
1½ teaspoons vanilla
Whipped cream

Place 3 cups milk in top of a double boiler and add half-and-half, butter, and ¾ cup sugar and stir. Cook until butter is melted and milk looks scalded.

In a bowl, whisk egg yolks until well broken up; then add ½ cup sugar and salt and whisk together very well. Slowly add this mixture to the hot milk mixture, stirring constantly. Stir for approximately ½ minute and then allow to cook for 15 to 20 minutes. (This gives the eggs time to cook and start the thickening process. Undercooking at this point slows the finishing process down by as much as half an hour.)

Mix 1 cup milk and cornstarch together and slowly add to the hot mixture. Be careful to stir constantly or lumps will form. Continue stirring for at least 2 minutes and every 5 minutes for the next 15 to 20 minutes.

When pudding is thick enough, stir in vanilla. Remove the whole double boiler from stove. (The hot water will help keep the pudding hot while you assemble the pies.)

Pour filling into pie shells. Fill pies so the tops are a little rounded. When cool, top with whipped cream. Makes 2 pies.

Metric Conversions

Volume Conversions

1 milliliter	=	slightly less than ¼ teaspoon
2 milliliters	=	slightly less than ½ teaspoon
5 milliliters	=	1 teaspoon
15 milliliters	=	1 tablespoon
59 milliliters	=	¼ cup
79 milliliters	=	⅓ cup
237 milliliters	=	1 cup
0.946 liter	=	4 cups = 1 quart
1 liter	=	1.06 quarts
3.8 liters	=	4 quarts = 1 gallon

Weight Conversions

28 grams	=	1 ounce
113 grams	=	4 ounces
227 grams	=	8 ounces
454 grams	=	16 ounces = 1 pound

Equivalent Measurements

3 teaspoons	=	1 tablespoon
4 tablespoons	=	¼ cup
5 tablespoons + 1 teaspoon	=	⅓ cup
8 tablespoons	=	½ cup
10 tablespoons + 2 teaspoons	=	⅔ cup
12 tablespoons	=	¾ cup
16 tablespoons	=	1 cup = 8 fluid ounces
2 cups	=	1 pint = 16 fluid ounces
4 cups	=	2 pints = 1 quart = 32 fluid ounces
2 quarts	=	½ gallon = 64 fluid ounces
4 quarts	=	1 gallon = 128 fluid ounces

Emergency Substitutions

Recipe results will vary when using substitutes. Use only in emergency circumstances.

Missing	Amount	Replace with
Powdered sugar	1 cup	1 cup granulated sugar + 1 teaspoon corn-starch, mixed in blender
Unsweetened chocolate	1 ounce	3 tablespoons cocoa powder + 1 table-spoon vegetable oil OR 1½ ounces bitter-sweet chocolate (remove 1 tablespoon sugar from recipe)
Bittersweet chocolate	1 ounce	4 tablespoons cocoa powder + 2 table-spoons butter OR ⅔ ounce unsweetened chocolate + 2 teaspoons sugar
Milk	1 cup	½ cup evaporated milk + ½ cup water OR ¼ cup nonfat dry milk + ⅞ cup water + 2 teaspoons butter
Buttermilk	1 cup	1 cup milk + 1 tablespoon lemon juice (stir together and let sit 5 minutes before use)
Whole milk	1 cup	⅝ cup skim milk + ⅜ cup half and half OR ⅔ cup 1% milk + ⅓ cup half and half OR ¾ cup 2% milk + ¼ cup half and half

Missing	Amount	Replace with
Half-and-half	1 cup	¾ cup whole milk + ¼ cup heavy cream OR ⅔ cup skim or lowfat milk + ⅓ cup heavy cream
Cornstarch (for thickening)	1 Tbsp	2 tablespoons flour
Flour (for thickening)	1 Tbsp	½ to ⅔ tablespoon cornstarch
Cake flour	1 cup	⅞ cup all-purpose flour + 2 tablespoons cornstarch
Self-rising flour	1 cup	1 cup all-purpose flour + 1½ teaspoons baking powder + ½ teaspoon salt
Baking powder	1 tsp	¼ teaspoon baking soda + ½ teaspoon cream of tartar

Index